Portrait of a Restaurant

Portsmouth

Portrait of a Restaurant

PORTSMOUTH

BRIAN R. SMESTAD

Blue Tree

PORTSMOUTH

First published in the United States in 2005
by Blue Tree, LLC.
P.O. Box 148
Portsmouth, NH 03802
www.thebluetree.com

37 10 1

Printed in Hong Kong

Library of Congress
Cataloging-in-Publication Data

Smestad, Brian.
    Portsmouth / Brian Smestad
Includes index.
ISBN 0-9711-3212-7
1. Portsmouth I. Title
2005908668

For customer service and orders:
Local 603.436.0831
Toll-Free 1.866.852.5357
Email sales@thebluetree.com

Blue Tree

For my Godfather Steve and Halle

MICHAEL GEHRON
GINO GULATTA
EVAN HENNESSEY
KEVIN MACDORMAND

KAREN LOGAN
SCOTT LOGAN
ROBERT WALKER

ELIZABETH GOVINI
MATT GOVINI

ELLEN BYRNE
CHRISTOPHER CARLSON

PENELOPE BREWSTER

RETCHARA PRADIT
RON PRADIT

GARY CARON

CHRIS HANSEN
JOE KELLEY
JEFF POLIZZO

PHELPS DIECK
DEB WEEKS

GARTH LYNDES
STEVE WYLER

MEREDITH STOLPER
LUIS GABRIEL VELEZ

BRUCE BELANGER
JOANNE HALL
GREG PIKE

THOMAS FIELDING
EVAN MALLET
SCOTT O'CONNOR

RAY GUERIN
MARK LIPONA

JACK BLALOCK
KEVIN WENTWORTH

JESSICA VASSILIOLN

DUNCAN BOYD

DAVID G. ROBINSON

43° North
Blue Mermaid
Breaking New Grounds
Byrne & Carlson
Ceres Street Bakery
Chiangmai
Dolphin Striker
Fat Belly's
Green Monkey
Harbor's Edge
Isis on Penhallow
Library Restaurant
Lindbergh's Crossing
Oar House
Old Ferry Landing
The Stockpot
Victory 96 State Street
Wellington Room

chapter one

SPRING

Blackberry Peach Oat Scones

4 CUPS FLOUR
2 CUPS OATS
½ CUP SUGAR
⅛ CUP BAKING POWDER
1 TEASPOON SALT
1 CUP FROZEN PEACHES CHOPPED
1 CUP FROZEN BLACKBERRIES
2 ¼ TEASPOONS CINNAMON
1 ½ TEASPOONS NUTMEG
¾ CUP HEAVY CREAM
4 EGGS
2 TABLESPOONS VANILLA
1 CUP UNSALTED BUTTER

Mix the flour, oats, sugar, baking powder, fruit, salt, cinnamon and nutmeg together.

Mix heavy cream, eggs and vanilla together and gently add to dry mixture.

Gently slice butter and add to the dough. Pat out to about 1-inch thickness. Cut into circles and bake on parchment paper at 350° until golden brown.

Ceres Street Bakery

Sticky Buns with Pecans

1 TEASPOON YEAST
½ CUP WARM WATER
1 CUP BROWN SUGAR
½ CUP SOUR CREAM
1 EGG YOLK
1 TEASPOON SALT
2 CUPS FLOUR
1 CUP BUTTER
1 CUP PECANS
2 CUPS FLOUR
CINNAMON

SERVES 6

Mix together yeast, warm water and brown sugar. Add sour cream, egg yolk, salt and flour and mix until smooth. Let rise until it doubles in size.

Place flour on countertop and roll dough into a 12x12-inch square. Spread ½ cup of butter and ½ cup of brown sugar over the square. Sprinkle with cinnamon and 1 cup of pecans. Roll and cut into 6 pieces.

Boil ½ cup of butter and ½ cup brown sugar and pour into an 8-inch round pan. Let cool for a few minutes. Arrange the dough spirals in the pan and let rise. Bake at 350° until golden brown.

Taos Bread

¼ CUP YEAST
1 ¼ CUPS BROWN SUGAR
3 ¾ CUPS WARM WATER
5 EGGS
2 ½ CUPS PUMPKIN
2 TABLESPOONS SALT
1 ¼ CUPS CORNMEAL
2 CUPS WHITE FLOUR

MAKES 3-4 LOAVES

Whisk together yeast, brown sugar and warm water and let expand. Add eggs, pumpkin, salt and cornmeal. Also add just enough white flour to knead into a smooth, elastic dough.

Let mixture expand to twice the size, knead it and divide into 3 or 4 pieces. Shape into loaves and let rise. Wash with egg.

Bake at 350°.

PANCAKES

4 CUPS ALL-PURPOSE FLOUR
2 TABLESPOONS BAKING POWDER
1 TABLESPOON BAKING SODA
1 TABLESPOON SALT
3 TABLESPOONS GINGER POWDER
1 TABLESPOON GROUND CINNAMON
½ TEASPOON GROUND CLOVES
3 LARGE EGGS
2 ½ OUNCES MOLASSES
3 CUPS BUTTERMILK
2 CUPS MILK
3 OUNCES MELTED BUTTER

LEMON AND HONEY SAUCE

1 CUP HONEY
1 LARGE LEMON

WHIPPED CREAM

1 CUP HEAVY CREAM
1 ½ TABLESPOONS CONFECTIONERY SUGAR
¼ TEASPOON VANILLA EXTRACT

SERVES 6

In a large bowl, sift together the flour, baking powder, baking soda, salt, ginger powder, cinnamon and cloves.

Whisk wet ingredients together and mix into sifted ingredients until combined.
Ladle ⅓ cup of batter onto a buttered, medium-high-heat griddle.

For the sauce, remove the zest from ½ of the lemon. Combine honey, lemon juice and zest in a small pot and heat until warmed.

For the whipped cream, whisk the cream in a bowl until thick, add sugar and vanilla extract.

1 THREE-POUND SALMON FILET, SKINNED AND DE-BONED
1 12 x 18-INCH PASTRY SHEET
5 OUNCES HERB GOAT CHEESE
1 CUP TOASTED PIGNOLIS
1 CUP LEEKS, SLICED AND RINSED
½ CUP SUN-DRIED TOMATOES, JULIENNED
1 EGG
SALT AND PEPPER

SERVES 5

SALMON EN CROUTE WITH HERB GOAT CHEESE AND PIGNOLIS

Lay pastry sheet on floured surface. Crumble goat cheese lengthwise across the center of the sheet. Place leeks and sun-dried tomatoes over cheese and add salt and pepper. Sprinkle with toasted pignolis nuts. Lay salmon lengthwise over cheese and vegetables.

Fold ends of pastry inward about 2 inches. Fold top and bottom of sheet together and overlap. Using 2 spatulas, 1 on each end, flip pastry over and place on parchment-lined baking sheet.

Beat egg and brush pastry with egg wash. Bake in 400° oven for 45 minutes or until golden.

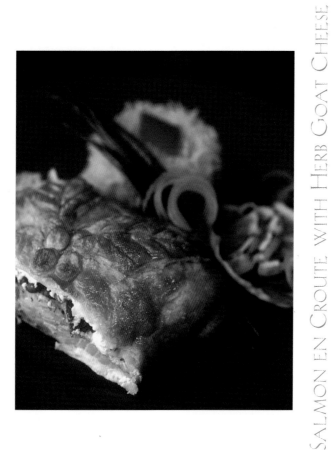

DRIED EGG WHITES
WATER
FINE GRANULATED SUGAR
PANSY OR OTHER EDIBLE FLOWERS

CRYSTALLIZED PANSY FLOWERS

Whisk a small portion of the dried egg with just enough warm water to create a paste. Holding the flower by the stem with tweezers, brush a small amount of paste over the entire flower. Be sure to paint underneath overlapping petals and inside any crevices.

Sprinkle the flower with just enough sugar to cover all of the egg whites. Lay face up on paper towels to dry.

Crystallized flowers kept in a dry, cool place will keep indefinitely. This recipe is best done on a dry day.

BYRNE & CARLSON

Chicken Satay

MARINADE

½ CUP COCONUT MILK
½ TEASPOON SALT
1 TABLESPOON SUGAR
1 TABLESPOON CURRY POWDER

CHICKEN

1 POUND CHICKEN BREAST, SKINLESS
CUT INTO LONG, THIN PIECES

SERVES 4

Mix marinade ingredients in a large bowl. Place chicken on bamboo skewers and leave in the marinade overnight.

Grill each piece of chicken for 5-10 minutes. Serve with peanut sauce and cucumber sauce.

Paradise Shrimp

14 SHRIMP
1 ONION, CHOPPED
1 FRESH PINEAPPLE
1 CUP TOMATO, DICED
1 CUP GREEN ONION, CHOPPED
1 EGG
1 CAN COCONUT MILK
1 TEASPOON CURRY POWDER
2 OUNCES RED CURRY PASTE

SERVES 2

Sauté curry paste over medium heat and stir. Add coconut milk and blend together thoroughly. Then add all of the vegetables and mix until it begins to boil. Let simmer and add the shrimp and egg into the pot. Stir well until fully cooked and ready to serve.

3 POUNDS PRINCE EDWARD ISLAND MUSSELS
2 CUPS DRY WHITE WINE
2 TABLESPOONS SHALLOTS, CHOPPED
1 TEASPOON SAFFRON
½ CUP CLARIFIED BUTTER
1 POUND CHORIZO SAUSAGE, GRILLED AND CHOPPED INTO
1-INCH PIECES
3 OUNCES LEEKS, JULIENNED
3 SLICES SOURDOUGH BREAD, GRILLED

SERVES 4

PRINCE EDWARD ISLAND MUSSELS

SERVED WITH GRILLED CHORIZO IN A WHITE WINE SAFFRON BROTH

In a large pot, sauté shallots in butter and add white wine, leeks, saffron, salt and pepper and the mussels.

Cover pot and simmer for 10-15 minutes or until the mussels open.

Arrange mussels symmetrically in a large bowl and pour broth over them. Garnish with grilled chorizo and sourdough points.

4 RIB CHOPS FROM A RACK OF VEAL, FRENCHED
10 OUNCES GLACE DE VEAU, HIGHLY REDUCED VEAL STOCK
2 OUNCES MADEIRA WINE
1 POUND ORGANIC KING OYSTER MUSHROOMS
1 TEASPOON GARLIC, CHOPPED
1 TEASPOON SHALLOTS, CHOPPED
KOSHER SALT AND PEPPER
4 OUNCES CLARIFIED BUTTER
1 OUNCE WHOLE BUTTER

SERVES 4

PAN-ROASTED VEAL CHOPS WITH OYSTER MUSHROOMS

Preheat oven to 450° and heat large sauté pan on the stove.

Season the veal chops liberally and sear in the pan with clarified butter until the chops are very brown on both sides. Place in roasting pan until all chops are seared. Set aside sauté pan and roast the veal in the oven with the mushrooms.

De-grease the sauté pan and sweat the shallot and garlic over low heat. Add the Madeira wine and reduce to a tablespoon. Then add the veal stock, bring to a simmer, season and swirl in the butter until emulsified. Strain.

Serve with garlic potatoes and sautéed asparagus.

RASPBERRY VINAIGRETTE

8 OUNCES RASPBERRY PUREE
2 TABLESPOONS RICE WINE VINEGAR
2 TABLESPOONS HONEY
½ TEASPOON GARLIC, CHOPPED
1 TABLESPOON BALSAMIC VINEGAR
½ CUP CANOLA OIL
WATER

PEARS

2 EACH, BOSC PEARS
¼ BOTTLE PORT WINE

SPICED PECANS

1 POUND PECAN HALVES
3 OUNCES HONEY
1 TABLESPOON SALT
½ TABLESPOON BLACK PEPPER
½ TABLESPOON CAYENNE PEPPER

SALAD

2 OUNCES BABY GREENS
1 OUNCE SUN-DRIED APRICOTS
2 OUNCES GORGONZOLA CHEESE, CRUMBLED
CANDIED GINGER

SERVES 4-6

For the raspberry vinaigrette, combine all ingredients, except oil and water in a food processor. Mix well and slowly add the oil and water until completely blended.

For the port wine poached pears, place peeled pears and port wine in a sauce pan and let simmer for 15 minutes. Let cool. Slice in half and de-seed the pear.

For the toasted spiced pecans, toss pecans, honey, salt, black pepper and cayenne pepper in a large bowl and mix together. Place mixture on a sprayed sheet pan and cook at 325°. Rotate and mix every 10 minutes. Let cook for approximately 30 minutes, or until caramelized.

For the salad, combine baby greens, apricots, gorgonzola cheese, toasted pecans, candied ginger and poached pears. Top with the raspberry vinaigrette and serve immediately.

GARLIC CONFIT

1 HEAD OF GARLIC
OLIVE OIL
SALT AND PEPPER
2 SPRIGS OF FRESH THYME

RED BEET EMULSION

2 MEDIUM-SIZED RED BEETS
2 CUPS OF PINOT NOIR
SALT AND PEPPER

RAMPS AND PEAS

½ POUND RAMPS
1 POUND OF ENGLISH PEAS

DUCK

2 DUCK BREASTS
SALT AND PEPPER
1 TABLESPOON OIL
2 ½ TABLESPOONS WHOLE BUTTER
½ TABLESPOON FRESH THYME LEAVES

SERVES 6

For the garlic confit, peel apart a head of garlic leaving the skins around each clove. Toss the cloves with a little olive oil, salt, pepper and fresh thyme. Loosely wrap in foil and cook in an oven at 350° for 30 minutes. Remove from the oven and allow to cool. Peel the skins off the cloves and store in an airtight container until ready for use.

For the red beet emulsion, place 2 red beets in a sauce pan with water and bring to a boil. Cover the pan and simmer until tender. Remove the beets and reserve the cooking liquid.

Peel the beets under cool water and set aside.

Strain the cooking liquid. Puree liquid with beets until mixture is smooth. Strain again until liquefied. Reduce 2 cups of Pinot Noir to ½ cup and add to the strained liquid. Season with salt and pepper. Transfer to a sauce pan and set aside.

For the vegetables, clean the ramps and cut the bottoms off, just above the root. Shell the English peas. Clean in cold water. Blanch the ramps in salted boiling water for about 10 seconds. Transfer to ice water then to paper towels and pat dry. Blanch the peas in boiling salt water for about 1 minute, transfer to ice water and drain excess water.

For the duck, score the skin of the duck into small diamond marks. Season with salt and pepper. On medium-low heat, render the fat from the skin. Once the skin is about ¼-inch thick, remove and place on paper towels to drain excess fat.

Grill the duck for 2 ½ minutes on each side. Remove and allow to rest.

In a sauté pan, heat 1 tablespoon of oil and ½ tablespoon of whole butter. Add the ramps, peas and garlic confit. Sauté for 1 minute, then add fresh thyme leaves, salt and pepper.

Heat the beet sauce to a simmer and whisk in 2 tablespoons whole butter, using an immersion blender to create bubbles.

Slice the duck into ⅛-inch-thick slices and set on top of the vegetables. Spoon the beet sauce around the plate and serve.

PLAINTAIN FRITTERS

2 WHOLE PLANTAINS, PEELED AND CHOPPED
1 CUP PINEAPPLE JUICE
1 TABLESPOON SUGAR
1 TEASPOON BAKING POWDER
1 CUP FLOUR

COCONUT CREAM SAUCE

2 TABLESPOONS COCONUT CREAM
2 TABLESPOONS COCONUT MILK
2 TABLESPOONS HEAVY CREAM

COD

2 OUNCES VEGETABLE OIL
4 EIGHT-OUNCE COD FILETS
2 CUPS CORN MEAL

SERVES 4

SERVED WITH PLANTAIN FRITTERS AND A COCONUT CREAM SAUCE

For the plantain fritters, process in roubo coupe plantains and pineapple juice until a thick paste forms.

Place into a mixing bowl and fold in the remaining ingredients.

With a 2-ounce ice cream scoop, place the fritters in a large pot and cook at 350° for 2 minutes or until golden brown.

For the coconut cream sauce, place 2 tablespoons of coconut cream, coconut milk and heavy cream in a sauce pan and reduce by ½. Serve warm with the plantain fritters.

For the cod, heat 2 saucepans with cooking oil for 2 minutes on medium heat.

Coat the cod with cornmeal and carefully place 2 cods in each pan. After 1 minute, flip the cod over and cook for another minute.

Place cod on an oiled sheet pan and place in the oven at 450° for 5 minutes.

Place the cod and fritters on the plate and top with the coconut cream sauce.

SAUTÉED SHRIMP

1 ½ WHOLE JALAPEÑOS, ROASTED AND SEEDED
3 TABLESPOONS ORANGE JUICE
¼ WHOLE ORANGE, ZEST AND JUICE
¾ CUP SOUR CREAM
½ CUP HEAVY CREAM
SALT AND PEPPER
3/8 TEASPOON TOASTED HERBS
16 JUMBO SHRIMP 21-25
2 POUNDS FETTUCCINE

SERVES 6

SERVED IN ORANGE JALAPEÑO CREAM SAUCE

Combine the jalapeños, orange juice, orange zest, sour cream, heavy cream, salt, pepper and spices in a large mixing bowl.

Heat the mixture in a sauté pan until reduced by ¼.

Sauté shrimp in vegetable oil for 3 minutes, stirring often.

Serve on fettuccine and garnish with an orange rind.

3 CUPS WHOLE MILK
1 CUP COCONUT MILK
½ CUP JASMINE RICE
½ TEASPOON SALT
½ CUP SUGAR
½ TEASPOON CINNAMON
¼ TEASPOON NUTMEG
½ CUP GUAVA PASTE
1 TEASPOON LIME ZEST

SERVES 8

Bruleed Guava Rice Pudding

Combine coconut and whole milk in a large bowl.

In a medium sauce pan, combine rice and 1 cup of the milk mixture. Bring to a simmer, stirring occasionally until the liquid is absorbed. Add the rest of the milk. Cook on low heat, stirring frequently for about 15 minutes.

Add all of the remaining ingredients except for the guava. Cool to room temperature. When cool, add guava chunks and then place into 8 ramekins or custard cups. Sprinkle with 1 tablespoon of sugar. Using a torch, hold fire close to the sugar in order to caramelize the sugar and obtain the brûlée crunch.

Isis on Penhallow

chapter two

SUMMER

VINAIGRETTE

½ CUP SUGAR
¼ CUP WATER
¼ CUP SHERRY VINEGAR
1 TABLESPOON RICE WINE VINEGAR
2 BLACK MISSION FIGS
½ VIDALIA ONION
½ TEASPOON GARLIC, MINCED
1 LEMON
2 TABLESPOONS DIJON MUSTARD
1 TEASPOON FRESH ROSEMARY, CHOPPED FINE
½ CUP OLIVE OIL
SALT AND PEPPER

SALAD

3 WHITE PEACHES, RIPE
1 LARGE BULB FENNEL, GREENS
1 VIDALIA ONION, SKINNED
1 HEAD CHICORY
3 FRESH BLACK MISSION FIGS
1 LEMON

SERVES 6-8

SUMMER WHITE PEACH AND FENNEL SALAD WITH FIG VINAIGRETTE

For the vinaigrette, place sugar, water, figs, vinegar, onions and garlic in a small, heavy sauce pan and simmer until they form a light syrup. Let cool.

In a food processor, blend egg yolk, lemon juice, mustard, rosemary, salt and pepper. While processing, slowly pour in fig syrup until smooth. Add the olive oil until the dressing is thick. Season to taste and refrigerate.

For the salad, shred the chicory into bite-size pieces and soak in cold water for 5 minutes. Remove the chicory and pat dry with a towel.

Slice fennel and onion as thin as possible. Cut the peach into half-moon slices. Toss peaches, onion and fennel in a mixing bowl with lemon juice and salt.

Toss the chicory in a large bowl with a generous amount of the dressing, and arrange neatly on chilled plates. Pile the peach salad on top of the chicory and garnish each plate with a half a fig.

Stockpot Lemonade

½ CUP ABSOLUT CITRON VODKA
2 CUPS SOUR MIX
½ CUP CRANBERRY JUICE
1 CUP CLUB SODA
1 LEMON

SERVES 4-6

Combine all ingredients in a large pitcher, then chill or fill with ice. Serve lemonade on the rocks and garnish with a lemon slice.

Vegetarian Rice Pilaf Salad

5 CUPS OF WATER
½ CUP VEGETABLE OIL
2 TABLESPOONS SALT
2 CUPS WHITE RICE
1 CUP DRIED BLACK EYE PEAS
1 CUP DRIED LENTILS
¼ CUP SUGAR
1 CUP DRIED CHIVES
2 TABLESPOONS CELERY SEED
2 TABLESPOONS BLACK PEPPER
2 TABLESPOONS GROUND CUMIN
2 TABLESPOONS MINCED GARLIC
2 TABLESPOONS OREGANO
1 CUP CIDER VINEGAR
1 CUP WHITE WINE WORCESTERSHIRE

SERVES 6

Combine rice, peas, and lentils with oil and salt in a 3-4 quart casserole or Dutch oven. Stir to coat with oil, then add water and stir. Cover tightly and bake at 400° for 45 minutes, or until all liquid is absorbed.

Whisk together the remaining ingredients. Add dressing to warm rice mixture and mix well.

Pilaf serves nicely over mixed greens or as a side dish.

SAUCE

1 CUP SOUR CREAM
1 MEDIUM CUCUMBER, PEELED AND CHOPPED
2 TABLESPOONS FRESH DILL, CHOPPED
2 TABLESPOONS FRESH LEMON JUICE
1 TEASPOON LEMON ZEST
¼ TEASPOON FRESH GROUND PEPPER

SALMON

4 SIX-TO EIGHT-OUNCE SALMON FILLETS

SERVES 6

Grilled Salmon with Cucumber-Sour Cream Sauce

Combine all sauce ingredients in a food processor and mix until smooth. Or, if you prefer a chunkier sauce, simply whisk ingredients together in a mixing bowl. Keep sauce refrigerated until ready to serve. Sauce can be made a day ahead.

Grill salmon over medium heat, 6-8 minutes each side until fish flakes with a fork. Drizzle salmon with sauce and serve with your favorite sides or over mixed greens.

SAFFRON BROTH

2 QUARTS FISH STOCK
1 TEASPOON SAFFRON
1 BUNCH CILANTRO
1 TEASPOON SPANISH PAPRIKA
1 BAY LEAF
3 GARLIC CLOVES
5 WHITE PEPPERCORNS

MONKFISH

2 ½–3 POUNDS MONKFISH, PEELED
1 ½ POUNDS BABY SQUASH
1 PINT CHERRY TOMATOES
½ BUNCH CILANTRO LEAVES
3 YUKON POTATOES

SERVES 4

POACHED MONKFISH IN CILANTRO AND SAFFRON BROTH

SERVED WITH BABY VEGETABLES

Combine ingredients for saffron broth in a pot on the stove top and heat to 200°. Strain 1 quart and reserve.

Clean and skin the monkfish tails or filets and cut into 4 portions. Poach in ½ cup unstrained saffron broth for 10 minutes or until firm to touch.

Blanch the squash until tender and strain. Cook the potatoes in salted water with a splash of vinegar until tender and strain. Combine the vegetables and place on 4 warmed soup plates. Garnish with cilantro leaves.

ISIS ON PENHALLOW

PINEAPPLE VINEGAR

2 QUARTS PINEAPPLE JUICE
1 QUART WHITE VINEGAR
8 GARLIC CLOVES
½ BUNCH OREGANO
½ BUNCH CILANTRO
1 BAY LEAF
¼ CUP SUGAR
7 WHOLE THAI CHILIES
1 TABLESPOON CAYENNE PEPPER
2 TABLESPOONS RED CHILI FLAKES
½ WHOLE FRESH PINEAPPLE

MUSSELS

5 POUNDS MUSSELS, WASHED
½ BUNCH CHERVIL
½ BUNCH TARRAGON
½ BUNCH CHIVES
½ BUNCH PARSLEY
3 TABLESPOONS CHOPPED GARLIC
¼ POUND BUTTER
1 TEASPOON CHILI FLAKES
2 CUPS PINEAPPLE VINEGAR
1 CUP WHITE WINE

STEAMED MUSSELS IN PINEAPPLE VINEGAR

Combine all of the pineapple vinegar ingredients in a large pot and let simmer for 15 minutes. Cool and put into a glass container and refrigerate for 5 days before using.

Chop the fresh herbs and mix with garlic, butter and chili flakes.

Heat butter and herb mixture in a large pot on high heat. Top with vinegar and wine. Cover the pot and steam the mussels for approximately 2-3 minutes or until the mussels have opened.

Serve mussels in large bowls with broth ladled over the top. Garnish with cherry tomato halves and sprigs of cilantro.

2 TABLESPOONS OLIVE OIL
1 MEDIUM WHITE ONION, DICED
2 RIBS CELERY, DICED
1 MEDIUM LEEK, DICED
1 TABLESPOON GARLIC, CHOPPED
1 TEASPOON FENNEL SEED
1 PINCH SAFFRON
1 CUP WHITE WINE
½ CUP PERNOD
1 ORANGE, JUICED
1 ORANGE ZEST
1 TABLESPOON OREGANO
1 TABLESPOON BASIL
2 BAY LEAVES
½ GALLON FISH STOCK
1 POUND CRUSHED TOMATOES
3 POUNDS FRESH MUSSELS
12 WHOLE CHERRYSTONE CLAMS
1 POUND FRESH MONKFISH, PEELED
2 WHOLE LOBSTERS
½ POUND LARGE SHRIMP, PEELED AND DEVEINED

SERVES 6

Sauté the onion, celery, leeks, fennel seed and garlic with the olive oil in a 1 gallon stock pot. Once the onions turn translucent, add the white wine and pernod. When the mixture begins to boil, add the remaining ingredients and let simmer for 20 minutes.

Place the lobsters on their backs and cut them lengthwise, starting at the head. Clean out the tomalley and roe from the lobsters. Place them in a separate pot with a little olive oil and the littleneck clams. Cover the pot and put on high heat. Once the clams begin to open, add the remaining seafood and the stock. Cover and let simmer for about 10 minutes.

When the mussels open and the remainder of the seafood is cooked, divide equally into large bowls and serve with French Bread.

RASPBERRY VINAIGRETTE

1 PINT FRESH RASPBERRIES
½ CUP RASPBERRY VINEGAR
1 CUP SALAD OIL
½ CUP SUGAR

SALAD

4 SEMI-BONELESS QUAIL
2 TABLESPOONS BALSAMIC VINEGAR
1 POUND MESCULIN MIX OR BABY GREENS

SERVES 4

GRILLED QUAIL SALAD WITH RASPBERRY VINAIGRETTE

Start by cutting the quail in half lengthwise. Marinate the pieces in the balsamic vinegar for a few minutes, then drain.

In a blender, mix raspberry vinegar, sugar, and a few whole fresh berries. Puree the mixture and then slowly add oil. Mix thoroughly and set aside.

Grill the quail a few minutes on each side. They will cook very quickly, so keep an eye on them.

In a mixing bowl, toss the greens with the vinaigrette. Place two halves of the cooked quail on top and garnish with fresh berries.

1 RACK OF LAMB, SPLIT IN HALF
3 TABLESPOONS DIJON MUSTARD
1 SPRIG OF FRESH ROSEMARY, CHOPPED
1 CUP FRESH BREAD CRUMBS
KOSHER SALT AND FRESH GROUND PEPPER
¼ CUP PORT WINE
2 CUPS WATER

SERVES 4

ROASTED RACK OF LAMB

In a small bowl, mix together the mustard, rosemary, salt and pepper. Rub the racks of lamb with the mixture and press with bread crumbs.

Preheat oven to 400°. Place the racks in a roasting pan and cook for 15 minutes. Remove from pan and let it rest for 10 minutes before slicing.

With the roasting pan still hot, discard the fat and pour in the port wine. Scrape the pan to release the flavor, then add the water. Let liquid reduce and serve as the sauce for the racks.

OAR HOUSE

New England Clam Chowder

1 MEDIUM ONION CHOPPED
3 STRIPS FATTY BACON DICED
2 MEDIUM POTATOES CUBED
2 CUPS CLAM JUICE
2 CUPS CHOPPED SEA CLAMS
½ TEASPOON OLD BAY SEASONING
2 CUPS CREAM OR MILK
SALT AND PEPPER
PAPRIKA

SERVES 6

Heat a 4-quart sauce pan over medium heat. Add diced bacon and cook until fat is liquid. (If bacon is not fatty, add vegetable oil). Then add chopped onions and stir until onions are coated. Add cubed potatoes and clam juice. Let simmer in covered sauce pan until potatoes are soft.

Add chopped clams and seasonings. Stir over medium heat for 5 minutes.

Pour cream or milk into 2-quart sauce pan over low heat and stir until warm.

When ready to serve, add cream to chowder base. Stir and ladle into bowls. Garnish with paprika.

New England Lobster Feast

1 LOBSTER PER PERSON, ANY SIZE
1 POUND MUSSELS PER PERSON
1-2 EARS OF CORN PER PERSON
1 POUND BUTTER
2 CUPS WHITE WINE
2 TABLESPOONS FRESH GARLIC, CHOPPED

Fill ⅔ of a large pot with water and bring to a boil. Place the lobster and corn in the pot and cook for approximately 8 minutes.

Place white wine and chopped garlic in another pot. Add mussels, cover and cook until wine foams to the top of the pot.

Heat butter in small saucepan until melted.

When all ingredients are prepared, place mussels onto large, individual plates and put the lobster and corn on top of the mussels.

Jumbo Shrimp and Fresh Lobster Meat

PESTO

¼ CUP PIGNOLIS
½ CUP FRESH PARMESAN CHEESE
4 ROASTED RED PEPPERS, WHOLE
1 BUNCH OF BASIL
½ CUP OLIVE OIL
SALT AND PEPPER

SHRIMP AND LOBSTER

12-18 JUMBO SHRIMP (8-12 SIZE), PEELED AND DEVEINED
2-3 POUNDS LOBSTER MEAT
2 TABLESPOONS BUTTER
2 TEASPOONS FRESH GARLIC, CHOPPED
2 CUPS HEAVY CREAM
5-7 RAVIOLI PER PERSON

SAUTÉED IN ROASTED RED PEPPER PESTO CREAM SAUCE

For the pesto, add pignolis, parmesan cheese, roasted red peppers and basil into food processor and begin blending. Slowly drizzle olive oil into the mixture until smooth and uniform. Add salt and pepper.

Bring large pot of water to boil for ravioli. Add pinch of salt or a splash of olive oil to water in order to prevent ravioli from sticking together. Cook ravioli for 5-7 minutes.

Melt butter in a large sauté pan on medium heat. Add shrimp and cook for 2 minutes. Flip shrimp with tongs and add cream. When cream heats up, add pesto. Mix together in the pan until uniform. Add lobster meat and cook for an additional 2 minutes.

Drain ravioli and place on a large serving dish with the sautéed shrimp and lobster. Garnish with fresh parmesan and parsley sprigs.

Old Ferry Landing

LEMON SAFFRON SABAYON

¼ CUP SAUTÉRN OR ANY DESSERT WINE
¼ CUP FRESH LEMON JUICE
1 TEASPOON SAFFRON THREADS
1 PINCH SALT
1 MEDIUM EGG
1 MEDIUM EGG YOLK
2 TABLESPOONS SUGAR
2 OUNCES COLD UNSALTED BUTTER,
CUT INTO ½-INCH CUBES

LOBSTER AND MELON SALAD

MEAT FROM 2 ONE-AND-ONE-HALF POUND LOBSTERS
1 CUCUMBER, PEELED
1 CHARANTAISE MELON, PEELED
1 TABLESPOON FRESH TARRAGON LEAVES
1 CUP LEMON SAFFRON SABAYON

SERVES 4

LOBSTER AND MELON SALAD IN LEMON SAFFRON SABAYON

For the lemon saffron sabayon, combine wine, lemon, saffron and salt in a non-reactive pan and simmer. Remove from heat and let steep for 5 minutes.

Whisk together the egg, egg yolk and sugar in a stainless bowl. Boil a small pot of water. Add the wine mixture to the egg mixture. Place bowl over a pot of water. Whisk mixture vigorously for 2-3 minutes until it thickens. Remove the bowl from the pot if it starts to get too hot.

When mixture is cooked, remove it from the heat and whisk in cold butter until completely blended. Push the warm sabayon through the fine strainer into the second bowl, place over ice and stir occasionally until cold.

Mix the lobster, diced melon, cucumber and tarragon leaves with about ⅓ of the sabayon, just enough to coat the diced ingredients.

Spoon the remaining sabayon evenly into 4 chilled serving plates and divide the salad evenly over the sauce. Garnish with thinly sliced melon and a small tarragon tip leaf.

2 TABLESPOONS OIL
1 STALK LEMONGRASS, DICED
4 LIME LEAVES, DICED
4 CHILI PEPPER, CHOPPED
1 ONION, CHOPPED
1 CUP SUMMER SQUASH
1 CUP CARROTS
1 CUP MUSHROOMS
1 CUP BABY CORN
½ CUP BASIL LEAVES
2 TABLESPOONS HOT AND SOUR CHILI PASTE

SEAFOOD

SHRIMP, MUSSELS, SCALLOPS OR SQUID

SERVES 4-6

SEAFOOD LEMONGRASS

In a pan, sauté onions, squash, carrots and baby corn. Add a little water and cook until vegetables are tender. Add seafood chili paste, chili pepper, lime leaves, lemongrass and basil leaves.

CHIANGMAI

GRILLED OR SEARED TUNA

SESAME MUSTARD SEED VINAIGRETTE

1 TABLESPOON TOASTED SESAME OIL
3 TABLESPOONS RICE WINE VINEGAR
1 TABLESPOON SOY SAUCE
2 TEASPOONS HONEY
1½ TEASPOONS GROUND DRY MUSTARD
1 CLOVE GARLIC, FINELY MINCED
1 TABLESPOON GINGER JUICE
1 TEASPOON GROUND BLACK PEPPER
½ CUP PEANUT OIL OR VEGETABLE OIL
1 TEASPOON WHOLE BROWN MUSTARD SEEDS, TOASTED

TUNA

1 POUND FRESH YELLOWFIN TUNA, CUT INTO 4 CUBES
1 TABLESPOON STAR ANISE, WHOLE
1 TABLESPOON CLOVES, WHOLE
1 TABLESPOON FENNEL SEED, WHOLE
1 TABLESPOON PEPPERCORN, WHOLE
1 TABLESPOON CORIANDER, WHOLE
1 TEASPOON GROUND CINNAMON
1 TEASPOON GROUND GINGER
1 TABLESPOON COCOA POWDER
1 TEASPOON SEA SALT
2 OUNCES WASABI PASTE
½ CUP YOGURT

SERVES 4

SERVED WITH SESAME MUSTARD SEED VINAIGRETTE
AND WASABI YOGURT

For the sesame mustard seed vinaigrette, combine all ingredients, except the peanut oil and whole mustard seeds, in a blender. While the blender is running, slowly add the oil to the mixture. When all of the oil is added and emulsified, add the mustard seeds and pulse the blender to mix them in without pureeing them. Refrigerate until needed.

Mix the yogurt and wasabi and set aside.

Sauté the greens with the vinaigrette until just wilted and warm.

For the tuna, toast the whole spices in a heavy pan over moderately high heat until fragrant. Grind the toasted spices and mix with the ground cinnamon, ginger, salt and cocoa.

Heat the grill pan. Coat the tuna cubes with the spice mixture and sear briefly on all sides.

Divide the greens among 4 serving plates, slice the tuna across the grain and arrange over the greens. Drizzle with remaining vinaigrette and wasabi yogurt. Sprinkle with sea salt.

CREME ANGLAIS

¼ QUART HEAVY CREAM
3 WHOLE EGG YOLKS
2 TABLESPOONS SUGAR
1 TEASPOON VANILLA

TARTS

8 WHOLE EGG YOLKS
14-OUNCE CAN SWEETENED CONDENSED MILK
16 OUNCE KEY LIME JUICE
1/8 CUP SUGAR
8 MINI GRAHAM CRACKER PIE SHELLS

SERVES 8

Combine all of the creme anglais ingredients into a mixing bowl and cook over a double boiler. Strain into a container and let cool.

In a mixing bowl, combine the egg yolks, condensed milk, and key lime juice. Mix until it turns into a smooth curd.

Lay out 8 mini pie shells onto a flat sheet pan.

Using a large ice cream scoop, place 1 scoop into each shell. Bake in a 350° oven for 15 minutes. Remove from the oven and let cool.

Drizzle creme anglais onto each plate and serve.

chapter three

Autumn

2 ¼ CUPS CAKE FLOUR
1 TABLESPOON BAKING POWDER
3 TABLESPOONS SUGAR
½ TEASPOON SALT
1 TEASPOON VANILLA
½ TEASPOON BAKING SODA
6 TABLESPOONS UNSALTED BUTTER
1 LARGE EGG
½ CUP HEAVY CREAM
½ CUP GOLDEN RAISINS
½ TEASPOON CINNAMON

CREAM SCONES WITH GOLDEN RAISINS AND CINNAMON

In a bowl, whisk together ½ cup of cream, egg, vanilla and 3 tablespoons of sugar.

In another bowl, combine flour, salt, cinnamon, baking powder and baking soda. Mix in the butter until completely blended. Then add the raisins and cream mixture. Mix with a fork until the mixture becomes dough.

Knead the dough gently on a floured surface for 30 seconds. Pat it into the desired size for each scone.

On a baking sheet, brush the scones with additional cream and sugar. Bake the scones at 400° for 15-18 minutes until they are golden brown.

6 POUNDS MUSSELS
1 STALK LEMONGRASS, MINCED
4 GARLIC CLOVES, MINCED
1 TABLESPOON GINGER, MINCED
¼ CUP SHERRY
1 TABLESPOON GREEN CURRY PASTE
2 TABLESPOONS SOY SAUCE
2 CANS COCONUT MILK
1 TABLESPOON GRAPESEED OIL

SERVES 4-6

MUSSELS

In a saucepan, sweat the lemongrass, garlic and ginger in grapeseed oil. Add the sherry and green curry paste and reduce heat. Add the coconut milk and soy sauce and let simmer for 30 minutes. The broth can be strained to remove the lemongrass. Ladle 4 ounces of the broth over fresh mussels and steam.

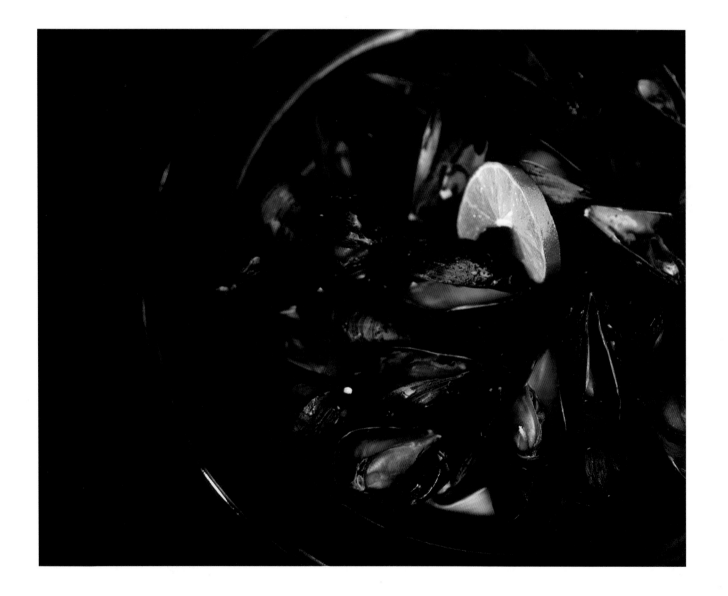

1 JALAPEÑO, DE-SEEDED AND DE-STEMMED
4 GARLIC CLOVES
2 TABLESPOONS CHILI GARLIC SAUCE
½ CUP MACADAMIA NUTS
1 LEMON ZEST
2 CUPS GRAPESEED OIL
½ BUNCH THAI BASIL
2 BUNCHES CILANTRO
SALT AND PEPPER

SERVES 4-6

ASIAN PESTO PAD THAI

Add all ingredients in a food processor and blend well. The pesto can be used with any asian noodle or vegetable. Serve hot or cold.

GREEN MONKEY

2 CUPS SHORT GRAIN WHITE RICE
1 LARGE SPANISH ONION, DICED
¼ CUP OLIVE OIL
3 CUPS WATER
½ TEASPOON SAFFRON
1 TEASPOON SALT
1 POUND CHORIZO SAUSAGE, CHOPPED
8 OUNCES SALMON, CUT INTO 1-INCH CUBES
8 OUNCES MONKFISH, PEELED AND CUT INTO 1-INCH CUBES
18-24 MUSSELS
3 BELL PEPPERS, DICED
2 POBLANO PEPPERS, DICED
2 LEEKS, CHOPPED
3 CUPS FISH STOCK OR VEGETABLE STOCK
1 TABLESPOON FRESH HERBS, CHOPPED
SALT AND PEPPER

SEAFOOD PAELLA

This recipe should be made in a paella pan, or paellera, now available in many specialty kitchen supply stores. A shallow wok will suffice, but the paella does not present itself as well in a wok.

For the rice, bring the water to a boil. Then sauté the onion and saffron in olive oil in a medium-sized pot. Add the rice, salt and saffron and stir. Pour the boiling water over the rice and cover with aluminum foil. Bring to a boil and let simmer. Check the rice in 15 minutes. When the grains are al dente, transfer rice to a sheet pan to cool.

Preheat oven to 450°.

Heat oil in a very large pan and add sausage. Season the fish cubes with salt and pepper and add them to the pan. Working quickly, turn heat to high and stir in vegetables and garlic.

When garlic is aromatic and fish is sticking to the pan, add partially cooked saffron rice and stir well. Add stock and herbs and bring to a boil.

Reduce the flame and stud the edges of the pan with mussels, hinge-end pointed down into the rice. There should be a generous amount of liquid in the pan. Cover the pan with foil or a lid until the mussels have opened. Take care that no rice is sticking to the bottom of the pan.

Remove lid and place in preheated oven for 10-15 minutes. (The paella is done when the rice turns brown and crispy around the edges of the pan. It can be held in a warm oven in this state for another 15 minutes if necessary.)

6 EIGHT-OUNCE BEEF FILET MEDALLIONS
¼ CUP PEPPERCORNS, COARSELY GROUND
2 TEASPOONS KOSHER SALT
¼ CUP OLIVE OIL OR CLARIFIED BUTTER
2 TABLESPOONS BRANDY
4 SHALLOTS, DICED
1 CUP HEAVY CREAM
1 OUNCE WHOLE UNSALTED BUTTER

SERVES 6

Preheat oven to 450°.

Sprinkle all surfaces of the filet medallions with salt. Then press the flat sides of the medallions into the pepper until both sides are well encrusted.

In a large sauté pan, sear the filets on all sides until dark brown. Remove the filets from the pan and place in a preheated oven, for about 8-10 minutes for medium rare.

Carefully deglaze the hot pan with brandy and add the shallots. When the alcohol has cooked off, add the demi-glace and simmer for 2 minutes. Pour in the cream and reduce by half.

Turn off the burner and add the herbs and butter. Adjust the seasonings and immediately pour over the filets.

TOMATO-VODKA SORBET

4 CUPS TOMATO JUICE
1 CUP SIMPLE SYRUP (COMBINE SUGAR AND WATER AND HEAT
TO DISSOLVE SUGAR IN A ONE TO ONE RATIO)
2 OUNCES VODKA
3 TABLESPOONS CILANTRO, MINCED

GAZPACHO

YELLOW TOMATO AND PINOT GRIGIO SAUCE
2 EACH, YELLOW TOMATOES
1 TABLESPOON WHOLE CORIANDER
1 TABLESPOON WHOLE CUMIN
2 STAR ANISE
1 SMALL-MEDIUM ONION, SLICED
OIL FOR COOKING
SALT AND PEPPER

GARNISH

1 SMALL RED ONION
1 SMALL ENGLISH CUCUMBER
1 YELLOW PEPPER
1 RED PEPPER

SERVES 4

GAZPACHO FRESCO ACCENTED WITH TOMATO SORBET

Combine all ingredients for the tomato-vodka sorbet in the bowl of your ice cream machine. Set according to the manufacturer's directions. It usually takes about an hour. Once completed, remove from your machine and put in the freezer.

In a heavy skillet, toast the cumin and coriander until fragrant, then add the onions and oil and sweat. Add the wine and simmer to reduce by ⅓.

In a blender, puree the yellow tomatoes. Once the wine is reduced, remove from the heat and add the puree. Let this mixture sit for 30-60 minutes.

Season with salt and pepper, strain through chinois and chill.

Place finely diced garnish into the middle of 4 chilled bowls. Ladle broths into bowls, topping with a scoop of sorbet.

AUTUMN '83

BASIL JUS

1 BUNCH BASIL
¼ CUP CHICKEN STOCK
SALT AND PEPPER
1 TABLESPOON FRESH LEMON JUICE

TOMATO OIL

1 CUP EXTRA VIRGIN OLIVE OIL
1 TABLESPOON TOMATO PASTE

FETTUCCINE

1 POUND FRESH EGG FETTUCINI
1 TABLESPOON SAFFRON

MUSHROOMS

3 PORTABELLO MUSHROOMS, JULIENNED
½ POUND SHIITAKE MUSHROOMS, JULIENNED
¾ POUND BUTTON MUSHROOMS, JULIENNED
1 CUP SHALLOTS, JULIENNED
FRESH THYME
SALT AND PEPPER

SCALLOPS

16 U8 SCALLOPS
1 BREASOLA APPLE, SLICED THIN
¼ POUND FRESH PECORINO, SLICED
2 POUNDS BABY SPINACH
½ CUP CHICKEN STOCK
SALT AND PEPPER
OIL FOR COOKING

SERVES 4

For the basil jus, combine the basil, chicken stock, salt, pepper and lemon juice in a blender and puree. Then chill.

For the tomato oil, combine 1 cup extra virgin olive oil and tomato paste in a blender and puree. Then chill.

For the fettuccine, bring a large pot of salted water to a boil. Crush saffron and add to the water. Let it steep as it comes to a boil. Once the water is boiling and deep in color from the saffron, add the pasta and cook until it is al dente. Drain and run under cool water. Toss with oil and refrigerate.

For the mushrooms, heat a large, heavy sauté pan over high heat. Add the shallots, mushrooms, salt, pepper, thyme and oil. Let sear, flip and cook until done. Remove and repeat until all of the mushrooms have been cooked.

For the scallops, pull away any abductor mussels attached to the scallops. Heat the oven to 450°.

Heat a sauté pan on high heat. Season the scallops with salt and pepper and place in the pan, adding some oil. Once seared, turn and top each scallop with a slice of apple and cheese. Place in oven to melt the cheese.

When scallops come out of the oven, transfer them to a plate and keep warm. Deglaze the pan with the chicken stock. Add the mushrooms, saffron fettuccine and spinach. Season and toss to just wilt the spinach.

Drizzle basil jus and tomato oil around each plate. Place pasta in the middle of each plate and four scallops around the pasta.

CARAMELIZED SHALLOT AND ROSEMARY-CRUSTED BEEF TORENADOS

SAUCE

2 TEASPOONS MINCED SHALLOTS
2 CUPS DEMIGLACE
1 CUP BORDEAUX WINE
4 OUNCES PORCINI MUSHROOMS, CHOPPED
4 OUNCES SHIITAKE MUSHROOMS, SLICED
SALT AND PEPPER

BEEF

8-4 OUNCE PETITE FILET
4 TABLESPOONS EXTRA VIRGIN OLIVE OIL
SALT AND PEPPER
16 LARGE SHALLOTS, PEELED AND SLICED
4 TABLESPOONS FRESH ROSEMARY, CHOPPED
4 TABLESPOONS SHERRY
3 DASHES WORCESTERSHIRE SAUCE
1 CUP PANKO CRUMBS
4 TEASPOONS PARSLEY, CHOPPED

SERVES 6

SERVED WITH A WILD MUSHROOM AND BORDEAUX DEMIGLACE

In a 12-inch sauté pan, heat olive oil over high heat.

Season filets with salt and pepper. Sear each filet for about 4 minutes on each side. Set on broiler pan.

Add shallots and mushrooms and sauté for 2 minutes.

Deglaze with wine and cook for 2 minutes. Add demiglace and reduce to medium heat for 5 minutes. Set aside.

Sauté shallots in butter over medium heat for 10 minutes or until they start to turn golden brown. Deglaze the pan with sherry, add rosemary, worcestershire sauce, salt, pepper and parsley. Add panko crumbs and stir.

Spread a thin layer of the mixture over each torenado.

Place under broiler on the middle rack for 5 minutes.

Reheat sauce, place torenados on the center of the plate and top with mushroom sauce.

Garnish with a fresh rosemary sprig.

½ POUND BLACK BEANS
1 WHOLE RED PEPPER, DICED
1 WHOLE GREEN BELL PEPPER, DICED
1 WHOLE POBLANO PEPPER, DICED
3 WHOLE JALAPEÑOS, DICED
1 CUP CORN, ROASTED
5 WHOLE CHIPOLTE CHILES, CHOPPED
1 WHOLE BERMUDA ONION, DICED
2 POUNDS GROUND BUFFALO
2 CANS TOMATOES, DICED
1 CAN CHILI SAUCE
½ CUP BROWN SUGAR
2 TABLESPOONS CUMIN
1 TABLESPOON KOSHER SALT
1 TABLESPOON BLACK PEPPER
2 TABLESPOONS CAYENNE
3 TABLESPOONS CHILI POWDER
1 TABLESPOON PAPRIKA
2 TABLESPOONS GROUND MUSTARD
1 ½ CUPS BOURBON WHISKEY
1 CUP MOLASSES
½ TIN TABASCO PEPPER SAUCE
2 TABLESPOONS GARLIC, CHOPPED
¼ CUP MALT VINEGAR

SERVES 10

Cook beans in 1 gallon of water until tender. Strain and let cool.

In a 5-gallon pot, sauté all vegetables in 2 tablespoons of oil until tender. Add buffalo meat and half of the bourbon to the vegetables. Do not drain.

Combine all other ingredients and simmer on medium heat for 3 hours.

GINGER MISO BUERRE BLANC

1 SHALLOT, MINCED
1 TABLESPOON GINGER, MINCED
2 GARLIC CLOVES, MINCED
2 CUPS SHERRY
1 TABLESPOON MISO PASTE
½ POUND BUTTER
1 CUP HEAVY CREAM

RED SNAPPER

2 POUNDS RED SNAPPER FILET
4 CUPS JAPANESE BREAD CRUMBS
1 TABLESPOON GINGER, MINCED
4 SCALLIONS, SLICED
SALT AND PEPPER
1 EGG
½ CUP OIL
¼ CUP MILK
2 CUPS SHIITAKE MUSHROOMS, SLICED
1 CUP CORN
1 CUP EDAMAME BEANS

SERVES 4

GINGER SCALLION CRUSTED RED SNAPPER

In a pan, add the shallot, ginger, garlic and sherry and reduce until the liquid has all been absorbed. Reduce the heat to low and whisk in the cold cubed butter. Once the butter has melted, add the cream, salt and pepper. The sauce can be strained for a smoother consistency.

Whisk the milk and egg together and set aside. Combine bread crumbs, garlic, ginger, scallions, salt and pepper in a bowl. Dip the flesh side of the fish into the egg mixture and then into the bread crumb mixture.

When all of the fish is breaded, heat a sauté pan with about ½ cup of oil. When the oil is hot, place the fish in the pan crumb side down until it is golden brown.

Remove the fish from the pan, then add mushrooms, corn, edamame beans, and sauté. Finish the fish in the oven at 350°. On a plate, ladle the ginger miso buerre blanc and place the fish on top of the sauce. Place the sautéed vegetables over the fish.

GREEN MONKEY

CRÈME BRÛLÉE

6 EGG YOLKS
¼ CUP SUGAR
2 CUPS HEAVY CREAM
3 TABLESPOONS CHAMBORD
1 PINT FRESH RASPBERRIES

SERVES 4

Gently heat the cream and chambord.

Whisk together the sugar and egg yolks for approximately 2 minutes. Slowly whisk the cream into the egg and sugar mixture. Pour the mixture into crème brûlée dishes.

Add the fresh raspberries into the dishes and bake in a water bath at 250° for about 1 hour until the brûlées have set.

Using a torch, hold fire close to the sugar in order to caramelize the sugar and obtain the brûlée crunch.

1 EIGHT-OUNCE CENTER CUT FILET MIGNON
OLIVE OIL
1/3 CUP CAPERS
1/3 RED ONION, MINCED
CRACKED BLACK PEPPER
REGGIANO PARMIGIANO
1 FRENCH BAGUETTE
PARCHMENT PAPER

SERVES 4

CARPACCIO OF BEEF TENDERLOIN

Wrap beef tightly in parchment paper, freeze, transfer to refrigerator 1 hour before serving.

Slice beef paper thin and arrange on dinner plate with pieces overlapping slightly. Sprinkle with capers, minced red onion and parmigiano cheese. Top with grilled croutons. Drizzle olive oil over the plate.

1 TWO-THREE POUND SUGAR PUMPKIN
1 MEDIUM YELLOW ONION, CHOPPED
4 CUPS CHICKEN STOCK
½ CUP HEAVY CREAM
1 LEMON
4 TABLESPOONS UNSALTED BUTTER
8 OUNCES FRESH LOBSTER MEAT
1 GRANNY SMITH APPLE
1 TABLSPOON FRESH CHIVES

SERVES 4-6

Sugar Pumpkin Soup with Lobster and Green Apple

To prepare the pumpkin, lay a folded damp dish towel on a cutting board. Break the stem off of the pumpkin, and with a large kitchen knife carefully split the pumpkin in half. Use a kitchen spoon to scoop out the pith and seeds.

Place the 2 halves, cut side down, on a cookie sheet and bake in a 350° oven for 30-40 minutes.

In a heavy soup pot, sauté the onion in 3 tablespoons of butter for 8-10 minutes and add the chicken stock.

Remove the pumpkin from the oven and let cool. Using a kitchen spoon, scrape the flesh from the skin and add it to the stock. Let simmer for 30 minutes.

Using a slotted spoon, remove the pumpkin and onion from the pot and place in a food processor. Add broth, 1 cup at a time until desired consistency is reached.

Discard any left-over broth and return the soup to the pot. Add heavy cream and lemon juice and season with salt and pepper. Reheat the soup to a simmer.

Peel and core the apple and cut into ¼-inch slices. Toss with remaining lemon juice.

Just prior to serving, melt the remaining tablespoon of butter in a small pan and add lobster meat and chives.

1 ½ POUNDS LARGE MONKFISH TAILS, CLEANED, PEELED AND
CUT INTO 1-INCH THICK MEDALLIONS
16 LITTLENECK CLAMS
6 OUNCES CHORIZO SAUSAGE, THINLY SLICED
1 RED BELL PEPPER, SEEDS AND PITH REMOVED
1 POBLANO CHILI, SEEDS AND PITH REMOVED
1 MEDIUM ONION, PEELED AND SLICED
6 GARLIC CLOVES, CHOPPED
4 TABLESPOONS EXTRA VIRGIN OLIVE OIL
3 FRESH BAY LEAVES
1 TABLESPOON PARSLEY, CHOPPED
1 TABLESPOON CILANTRO, CHOPPED
1 CUP WHITE WINE

SERVES 4

PORTUGUESE-STYLE MONKFISH WITH CLAMS

In a large, heavy skillet, add olive oil on low heat. Allow oil to heat up and add bay leaves, garlic and chorizo until the garlic turns brown. Add the peppers, onion and tomato. Increase the heat to medium and sweat the vegetables and chorizo for 8-10 minutes.

Arrange the monkfish and clams in a single layer on top of the vegetables. Add the wine and cover for 15 minutes.

When the monkfish is cooked and the clams are open, sprinkle with parsley and cilantro.

Serve with roasted potatoes and crusty bread.

MOUSSE

8 OUNCES BITTERSWEET CHOCOLATE, BROKEN
2 TABLESPOONS UNSALTED BUTTER
4 LARGE EGGS
1 CUP SUGAR
⅔ CUP HEAVY CREAM
2 TABLESPOONS COCOA POWDER
1 TEASPOON SALT

CARAMELIZED PEARS

4 SEMI-RIPE PEARS (STILL FIRM),
PEELED AND CUT INTO QUARTERS LENGTHWISE
1 CUP RAW SUGAR
2 TEASPOONS UNSALTED BUTTER
4 TABLESPOONS HAZELNUT PRALINE COARSELY CHOPPED

SERVES 4

BITTERSWEET CHOCOLATE MOUSSE

SERVED WITH ROASTED PEARS AND HAZELNUT PRALINE

Melt the chocolate and butter in a double boiler, until completed mixed and set aside.

In a mixer, whip together eggs and sugar for about 4-8 minutes until fluffy.

Fold half of the whipped eggs into the chocolate. Then fold the remaining half into the mixture.

In mixer, whip heavy cream until it forms sofy peaks. Mix into chocolate.

Sift 2 tablespoons cocoa powder and 1 teaspoon of salt on top of the chocolate and fold into the mixture.

Cover and chill mousse for at least 2 hours before serving.

For the caramelized pears, toss the pears into a bowl with raw sugar and mix until the pears are well coated.

In a heavy 2-quart, flameproof casserole dish, melt butter on medium-high heat. Add pears in a single layer until they turn brown on both sides. Continue turning the pears until the color is even.

Ladle some of the pears and caramel sauce into wide soup bowl. Place the mousse on top of the pears and serve with chopped pralines.

chapter four

WINTER

2 ¼ ALL-PURPOSE FLOUR
1 ½ TEASPOONS BAKING POWDER
¼ TEASPOON SALT
¾ CUP SUGAR
½ CUP UNSALTED BUTTER
2 LARGE EGGS
1 CUP WALNUTS, COARSELY CHOPPED
6 OUNCES BITTERSWEET CHOCOLATE, CHOPPED

MAKES 3 DOZEN

CHOCOLATE-WALNUT BISCOTTI

In a medium bowl, whisk flour, baking powder and salt.

Using an electric mixer, beat sugar and butter in a large bowl. While blending, add 1 egg at a time. Then add the flour to the mixture. Stir in the walnuts and chocolate.

Divide the dough in half, wrap in plastic and freeze for 20 minutes until it is firm.

Preheat oven to 350°. Line a large baking sheet with parchment paper.

Using flour to prevent the mixture from sticking, divide the dough into 14-inch long, 2 ½ inch wide pieces. Place each piece on the baking sheet 2 ½ inches apart. Bake for 30 minutes until golden brown. Let cool for 20 minutes.

Using a serrated knife, cut the biscotti on a diagonal into ½ inch-thick slices. Stand slices upright on the baking sheet.

Bake biscotti for 30 minutes until dry to touch and pale golden. Cool completely before serving.

SYRUP

4 LARGE CALMYRNA OR BROWN TURKEY FIGS
1 CUP MARSALA
½ CUP WILDFLOWER HONEY
SEA SALT
6 PEPPERCORNS
6 WHOLE CLOVE

MARSALA

FRESH GOAT CHEESE
2 TABLESPOONS WILD FLOWER HONEY
1 TEASPOON SEA SALT
2 TABLESPOONS HEAVY CREAM
4 OUNCES 74-76% BITTERSWEET CHOCOLATE
1 OUNCE COLD UNSALTED BUTTER
PINCH SALT
PHYLLO DOUGH, CUT INTO 4-BY-4-INCH SQUARES 3 LAYERS EACH

SERVED WITH CHOCOLATE PURSE AND HONEYED GOAT CHEESE

Bring all of the syrup ingredients, except for the figs, to a simmer in a small pot. Then add the figs and cover loosely.

Reduce heat and cook gently for approximately 6-7 minutes. Remove pot from heat, careful not to rupture the delicate skins of the figs. Allow figs to cool in their poaching syrup.

Refrigerate cooled figs. Strain syrup and return it to a simmer. Gently reduce by half.

Whip together goat cheese, honey, sea salt and heavy cream until smooth. Transfer to a bowl and place in the freezer until very firm but not frozen.

In a double boiler, melt the chocolate, butter and salt. Transfer to an ice bath to cool completely. Form the resulting ganache into 4 equal balls and freeze.

To prepare the phyllo squares, take 1 sheet of phyllo and lay it on a moist towel. Brush with clarified butter 6 times. Cut the finished sheet into 4x4 inch squares.

Place 1 ganache ball in the center of each phyllo square. Moisten 2 adjoining edges and bring the opposite edges over to form a triangle out of each square. Chill.

When ready to serve, bake the phyllo purses in a 400° oven for 6-7 minutes. Arrange one fig, one scoop of goat cheese and 1 phyllo packet on each plate. Drizzle with reserved syrup. Serve immediately.

GLAZE

1 ½ CUPS APRICOT PRESERVES
6 OUNCES MANGO CHUTNEY
1 TEASPOON GARLIC, CHOPPED
2 TABLESPOONS CRYSTALLIZED GINGER, MINCED
2½ TABLESPOONS SOY SAUCE

PORK

4 PER-PERSON, PORK TENDERLOIN, CLEANED
2 TABLESPOONS DARK CHILI POWDER
1½ TABLESPOONS SWEET PAPRIKA
1½ TABLESPOONS CUMIN, GROUND
1½ TABLESPOONS CORIANDER, GROUND
½ TABLESPOON BROWN SUGAR
¼ TABLESPOON OREGANO
1 TEASPOON BLACK PEPPER
1½ TABLESPOONS GARLIC, MINCED
3 OUNCES CINNAMON

SERVES 6

SPICED PORK TENDERLOIN WITH A WESTERN APRICOT GLAZE

For the western apricot glaze, combine all of the ingredients in a sauté pan and let simmer for 10 minutes. Let cool slightly, then burr mix with a hand mixer.

For the meat, mix together all of the ingredients and spread evenly on the pork tenderloin. Let the pork sit for about 1 hour. Bake at 350° for approximately 15-20 minutes. Pork is done when the temperature reads 140° for medium and 150° for medium well.

Serve with rice pilaf.

FAT BELLY'S

SAUCE

3 OUNCES WHITE LEEKS
1 TABLESPOON GARLIC, CHOPPED
3 CUPS CHICKEN BROTH
1 QUART HEAVY CREAM
5 ½ OUNCES V8 JUICE
¼ CUP CORNSTARCH
1 CUP WATER
1 POUND MAYTAG BLUE CHEESE
SALT AND BLACK PEPPER

BREAD

4 PIECES FOCCACIA BREAD
1 TABLESPOON GARLIC, CHOPPED
2 OUNCES WHOLE BUTTER, MELTED

SERVES 4-6

For the maytag sauce, sauté leeks and garlic on low heat for approximately 5 minutes in order to caramelize. Add chicken broth and reduce by half. Add heavy cream and again reduce by half. Add V8 juice and slowly mix in the cornstarch slurry. Let simmer for 5 minutes. Remove from the heat and add the maytag blue cheese. Season with salt and pepper.

For the bread, combine chopped garlic with melted butter. Brush fresh foccacia bread with garlic butter and grill until lightly toasted.

Heat up the maytag sauce and ladle on the plate. Arrange bread over sauce as desired and serve.

1 TABLESPOON CHOPPED FRESH TARRAGON
1 MINCED SHALLOT
1 TEASPOON CRACKED PEPPER
1 CUP RED WINE VINEGAR
16 JUMBO SHRIMP, SHELLED AND CLEANED
2 POUNDS BEEF TENDERLOIN TIPS
SALT AND WHITE PEPPER
CAYENNE PEPPER
4 EGG YOLKS
1 POUND UNSALTED BUTTER, SOFTENED

SERVES 4

LAND AND SEA WITH SAUCE BERNAISE

For the sauce bernaise, combine tarragon, shallots, cracked pepper and vinegar in a saucepan. Bring to a boil and let simmer until reduced to 1/16 cup.

Place egg yolks in stainless steel bowl with 1 tablespoon cool water and whisk vigorously over medium heat until it thickens. Add the butter, just a few slices at a time until all the butter is incorporated. Then add salt, cayenne and tarragon reduction.

Using eight skewers, divide the beef and shrimp into eight portions. Brush lightly with softened butter and season with salt and pepper. Grill beef and shrimp to desired temperature.

Place a skewer of beef and a skewer of shrimp on each dinner plate and top with the bernaise sauce.

MINTED BLACKBERRY GLAZE

½ PINT BLACKBERRIES
¼ CUP HONEY
½ CUP MINT LEAVES

BALSAMIC REDUCTION

4 CUPS BALSAMIC VINEGAR

SWEET POTATO FENNEL MOUSSE

1 CUP PECAN WOOD CHIPS, SOAKED IN WATER
1 HEAD FENNEL
1 MEDIUM ONION
2 POUNDS SWEET POTATO, ROASTED
SALT AND PEPPER

ASPARAGUS AND EGGPLANT

12 PIECES ASPARAGUS
½ EGGPLANT
SALT AND PEPPER

DUCK

4 LONG ISLAND DUCK BREASTS
2 CUPS CHICKEN STOCK
¼ CUP BUTTER, CUT INTO CUBES
SALT AND PEPPER

SERVES 4

ROAST DUCK BREAST WITH PECAN SMOKED SWEET POTATO FENNEL MOUSSE

Served with grilled marinated eggplant

For the minted blackberry glaze, combine all of the ingredients into the food processor and puree.

For the balsamic reduction, in a small sauce pan bring the vinegar to a boil and let simmer until it is thick and syrupy.

For the sweet potato and fennel mousse, set smoker and drain water from the wood chips. Make the chips smolder and place the fennel and onions into the smoker. Seal the smoker for 45 minutes.

Once the fennel and onions are smoked and the potatoes are roasted, puree each separately in a food processor and then mix together. Keep warm or refrigerate until needed.

Note: If you do not have a smoker, you can roast all of the ingredients in a 350° oven until tender. Then add a teaspoon of liquid smoke to the puree. Be careful with liquid smoke because it is very potent.

For the grilled asparagus and eggplant, boil a large pot of heavily salted water and heat the grill. Slice eggplant into 1-inch sections and salt heavily to remove moisture and bitterness. Place the asparagus in the boiling water. When the water returns to a boil, place the asparagus in an ice water bath, then drain and dry.

When the eggplant is no longer moist, brush off the salt and season with salt and pepper. Place on the grill until it is almost cooked and then remove and let cool. Dice the eggplant into ¼-inch pieces. Place the asparagus, seasoned with salt and pepper on the grill just long enough to heat it.

For the duck, heat the oven to 450°. Using a sharp knife, score the fat on the duck in a diamond pattern. Heat a sauté pan over low heat. Season the duck with salt and pepper on both sides. Lay the breasts in the pan, skin side down, and render the fat until crispy. Turn the duck, brush with blackberry glaze and put in the oven. For medium rare, cook 4-5 minutes.

When the duck comes out of the oven, remove it from the pan and let the meat rest while you prepare the jus. Pour the fat out of the pan and deglaze it with chicken stock. Mix in the butter and fresh herbs.

YELLOWFIN TUNA WITH HERBED GNOCCHI

6 SIX-OUNCE YELLOWFIN TUNA

GNOCCHI

2 ½ POUNDS RUSSET POTATOES
1 ¼ CUPS ALL-PURPOSE FLOUR
2 TABLESPOONS FRESH TARRAGON, CHOPPED
2 TABLESPOONS FRESH CHIVES
2 TABLESPOONS FRESH THYME
¼ CUP MASCARPONE CHEESE
SALT AND PEPPER
8 QUARTS SALTED WATER

MUSHROOMS AND SQUASH

½ POUND MUSHROOMS
1 WHOLE BUTTERNUT SQUASH
4 GARLIC CLOVES, SLICED
FRESH THYME SPRIGS
OLIVE OIL FOR COOKING
SALT AND PEPPER

CARROT-TARRAGON PUREE

4 MEDIUM CARROTS
4 SPRIGS TARRAGON
1 SPRIG THYME

SERVES 6

Serverd with roasted organic chestnut mushrooms, butternuti squash, and carrot-tarragon puree

For the potato gnocchi, bake Russet potatoes at 450° until tender in the middle. Remove from oven and allow to cool. Cut the potatoes in half and scoop out the inside. Place all the insides into a potato ricer or food mill and grind the potato.

Put the ground potato in a mixing bowl and sift in 1 ¼ cups of all-purpose flour. Add fresh tarragon, chives and thyme. Also add ¼ cup of mascarpone cheese, salt and pepper. Using your hands, gently kneed the dough together, being careful not to over work the gluten in the flour and starch in the potato. Once dough starts to push back, allow it to rest for 20 minutes. Using a knife, cut the dough every ½ inch to make cylinders. Dust with flour so the pieces do not stick together.

Bring 8 quarts of salted water to a boil and poach the gnocchi until firm and floating. Remove gnocchi and place in an ice bath to cool. Once they are cold, coat lightly with oil. Keep in an airtight container until ready for use.

For the mushrooms and squash, trim the mushrooms at the bottom of the stems, toss with olive oil, salt, pepper, garlic cloves, fresh thyme. Roast in a 450° oven for about 10-12 minutes. Remove and allow to cool. Dice the squash into ¼-inch cubes. Bring a pot of salted water to boil and blanch the squash for about 3-4 minutes until it is tender. Remove and allow to cool.

For the carrot-tarragon puree, peel and dice carrots into ¼-inch cubes. Bring water to a boil and blanch the carrots until they are soft. Remove from heat and mix in tarragon and thyme. Cover and let steep for 10 minutes. Remove tarragon and thyme. Puree using a hand-held blender. Season with salt and pepper. Keep warm until ready for use.

For the tuna, season fish with salt and pepper and sear on both sides until golden brown. Remove the tuna. Using the same pan, sauté the gnocchi until golden brown. Add mushrooms and squash. Sauté for another minute and season with salt and pepper.

In the center of each plate, make a ring of the puree and place some of the gnocchi mixture on top. Cut the tuna into ¼-inch slices and fan over the gnocchi and serve.

VINAIGRETTE

½ CUP NICOISE OLIVES, PITTED
3 TABLESPOONS RED WINE VINEGAR
½ CUP OLIVE OIL
1 TABLESPOON GARLIC, DICED
SALT AND PEPPER

TOMATO CONFIT

3 TOMATOES
3 SPRIGS OF THYME
3 GARLIC CLOVES
3 SHALLOTS
OLIVE OIL

ARTICHOKES

2 LARGE ARTICHOKES
1 QUART WATER
1 QUART WHITE WINE
4 SPRIGS OF THYME
1 CARROT, PEELED AND DICED
3 SHALLOTS
2 BAY LEAVES
1 TABLESPOON BLACK PEPPERCORN
3 TABLESPOONS OLIVE OIL

RED SNAPPER

20 OUNCES FLORIDA RED SNAPPER
SALT AND PEPPER
OIL FOR COOKING
CAPERBERRIES
PISTACHIOS

SERVES 4

SERVED WITH FINGERLING POTATOES, TOMATO CONFIT, TOASTED PISTACHIOS, CAPER BERRIES, GRILLED ARTICHOKES AND A NICOISE OLIVE VINAIGRETTE

For the nicoise vinaigrette, blend the nicoise olives with red wine vinegar, olive oil and diced garlic. Season with salt and pepper. Chill before use.

Toss the pistachios with oil and a pinch of salt. Toast at 450° for about 4-5 minutes until fragrant. Once toasted, remove to a paper towel to drain excess oil. Slice the caperberries in half and set aside.

For the tomato confit, score the tops of the tomatoes. Place in a 4-inch-deep oven-proof container with thyme, garlic cloves and shallots. Cover with olive oil then with foil. Cook in a 350° oven for about 45 minutes until the skins start to peel off. Remove from the oil and allow to cool.

Cut the tomatoes into quarters, remove the seeds and peel off the skins. Set aside.

For the artichokes, trim the tops of the leaves and around the base. Place into a poaching liquid made up of 1 quart water, 1 quart white wine, 4 sprigs of thyme, 1 carrot, 3 shallots, 2 bay leaves, 3 tablespoons olive oil and 1 tablespoon black peppercorn. Bring to a simmer and cover. Cook for 1 hour until tender. Remove and cut into quarters.

Portion the fish into 5-ounce pieces. Using the back of the knife, scrape any excess water or scales off of the skin.

Season with salt and pepper. Sear the fish skin-side first, in a sauté pan with oil on high heat until golden brown. Flip the fish over and finish cooking in a 350° oven for 4 minutes. Remove and place on a paper towel to drain excess oil.

Sauté the fingerlings until golden brown. Then add the tomato confit and pistachios. Sauté for about 30 seconds and toss in caperberries and season with salt and pepper.

Cut the artichokes in half and grill on both sides until they are hot in the center.

Spoon the tomato mixture onto the middle of each plate and top with a piece of fish. Pour the vinaigrette over the dish and serve.

43° NORTH

1 CUP HEAVY CREAM
12 OUNCES BITTERSWEET CHOCOLATE (60-65% COCOA)
1 CUP PITTED PRUNES, SOAKED IN ARMAGNAC FOR 2 DAYS
1/3 CUP ARMAGNAC
1 POUND COCOA POWDER
4 TABLESPOONS SMOKED SPANISH PAPRIKA
1 POUND BITTERSWEET CHOCOLATE

SERVES 6

Boil heavy cream in the sauce pan, whisking occasionally.

In the food processor, finely chop 12 ounces of chocolate. While blending, add the hot cream. When all the cream has been added, turn off the food processor and let the mixture sit for 30 seconds. Then process just long enough to create a smooth ganache. Scrape ganache into the mixing bowl.

Add the prunes to the food processor and pulse until coarsely ground. Add ⅓ cup of armagnac. Scrape the prune mixture into the ganache and fold in with a spatula. Cover and refrigerate over night.

The following day, remove the ganache from the refrigerator and scrape the surface with a stiff spatula; if too firm, allow to sit at room temperature. Roll the ganache into quarter-sized balls.

On a baking sheet, sift the cocoa powder with the paprika.

Melt 1 pound of bittersweet chocolate in the double boiler. Immediately remove from hot water, being careful not to get any water into the melted chocolate. Let cool, mixing occasionally.

Gently hand coat each truffle with a thin shell of chocolate and drop into cocoa powder mixture. Before the chocolate hardens, roll the truffle through the cocoa to cover completely. Set aside to cool at room temperature.

VARIETY OF LIQUEURS CAN BE USED:
CAMPARI, PERNOD, LIMONCELLO, PORT OR SHERRY
2 POUNDS SUGAR
1 POUND LIGHT CORN SYRUP
1 CUP WATER
QUICK-SET PECTIN POWDER MIXED WITH SUGAR
1 ½ CUPS LIQUEUR
1 OUNCE CITRIC ACID SOLUTION

MAKES 100-150 PIECES

APERITIF JELLIES

In a large sauce pan, combine sugar, corn syrup and water. Heat on medium high until liquefied. Gradually whisk in pectin and sugar mixture. Heat until thermometer reads 226°, then gradually add the liqueur. Continue cooking until the thermometer again reaches 226°.

Remove from heat and add citric acid solution. Combine thoroughly. Quickly pour the jelly onto the baking sheet. Let it cool, then cut into squares and toss in granulated sugar.

Store in an airtight container and consume within one month.

I would like to thank the following people who have contributed in some way to this project. It was with their help and support that this book became possible.

LUKAS ALONSO

REBECCA CROWLEY

MEREDITH BLAKE

KELLY MULLEN WEISER
PAOLO WEISER

MICHAEL PENNY
MIGUEL'S COLOR SERVICE

MONTAGE GRAPHICS

ALISON VOLK

PATRICIA BLAKE

ADRIAN DAVIS
JAIMIE LAFLUER
CHRIS PRYOR
LIZA SATURLEY
GALEN SATURLEY

RICHARD JOSEPH
GEOFF HOLMES
TIFFANY HOWE
BRENDAN CORNWELL

KELLY MULLEN WEISER
PAOLO WEISER

VIDA HOLLANDER

MARGARET HOLLANDER
BILLY HOLLANDER

ELIZABETH D. CHICKNAVORIAN
BOB WINCHESTER

CONSTANCE S. WARREN
WILLIAM T. WARREN

43° NORTH 75 Pleasant Street

BLUE MERMAID The Hill

BREAKING NEW GROUNDS 14 Market Square

BYRNE & CARLSON 121 State Street

CERES STREET BAKERY 15 Penhallow Street

CHIANGMAI 128 Penhallow Street

DOLPHIN STRIKER 15 Bow Street

FAT BELLY'S 2 Bow Street

GREEN MONKEY 86 Pleasant Street

HARBOR'S EDGE 250 Maket Street

ISIS ON PENHALLOW 106 Penhallow Street

LIBRARY RESTAURANT 401 State Street

LINDBERGH'S CROSSING 29 Ceres Street

OAR HOUSE 55 Ceres Street

OLD FERRY LANDING 10 Ceres Street

THE STOCKPOT 53 Bow Street

VICTORY 96 STATE STREET 96 State Street

WELLINGTON ROOM 67 Bow Street